Love

'Challenging our cultural narrative that love is a "feeling", this rich devotional invites you to explore the nature of the love of God as a hallmark of discipleship. Easy to access and full of biblical truth, this little book will both nourish your soul and challenge you to live differently for the kingdom.'
Katharine Hill, author, speaker and UK Director, Care for the Family

'If *love* is the most valuable of things, it is also the most misunderstood, confused, corrupted and obstructed. This book is a wonderful resource to aid us all in both understanding and living out this most vital of words. It is deeply rooted in Scripture, rich in application and simultaneously thought-provoking and heart-warming. I recommend it enthusiastically.'
J.John, author and speaker

30-DAY DEVOTIONAL

Love

Edited by Elizabeth McQuoid

Keswick
Resources

FOOD
FOR THE
JOURNEY

INTER-VARSITY PRESS
36 Causton Street, London SW1P 4ST, England
Email: ivp@ivpbooks.com
Website: www.ivpbooks.com

First published 2022

British Library Cataloguing-in-Publication Data
A catalogue record for this book is available from the British Library.

ISBN: 978–1–78974–198–8
eBook ISBN: 978–1–78974–197–1

Set in Avenir 11/15 pt
Typeset in Great Britain by CRB Associates, Potterhanworth, Lincolnshire
Printed in Great Britain by Clays Ltd, Elcograf S.p.A.

Produced on paper from sustainable sources

Inter-Varsity Press publishes Christian books that are true to the Bible and that communicate the gospel, develop discipleship and strengthen the church for its mission in the world.

IVP originated within the Inter-Varsity Fellowship, now the Universities and Colleges Christian Fellowship, a student movement connecting Christian Unions in universities and colleges throughout Great Britain, and a member movement of the International Fellowship of Evangelical Students. Website: www.uccf.org.uk. That historic association is maintained, and all senior IVP staff and committee members subscribe to the UCCF Basis of Faith.

Contributors

Ruth 1:1 – 4:22
Rico Tice
Rico is Senior Minister (Evangelism) at All Souls Church, Langham Place in London. He is the co-founder of Christianity Explored Ministries. He has written a number of books, including *Honest Evangelism*, *Capturing God* and *Faithful Leader*.

Hosea 10:1 – 11:11 and Romans 8:31–39
Vaughan Roberts
Vaughan has been Rector of St Ebbe's Church, Oxford, since 1998. He is the author of many books, including *God's Big Picture: A Bible Overview* and *Battles Christians Face*.

Matthew 5:43–48
David Coffey
David was the General Secretary of the Baptist Union of Great Britain for fifteen years. He then became President of the Baptist World Alliance and is now the Global Ambassador for BMS World Mission.

Mark 12:28–34
Martin Salter
Martin is Lead Pastor at Grace Community Church, Bedford. He is a trustee of and speaker at the Keswick Convention, and author of *Mission in Action* and *So Loved*.

John 13:1–38
Derek Tidball
Derek served as the pastor of two Baptist churches and as the Principal of the London School of Theology for twelve years. He now teaches in various colleges, including Spurgeon's, Moorlands and the South Asia Institute of Advanced Christian Studies (Bangalore). He has written many books, including a number of commentaries in IVP's The Bible Speaks Today series.

John 21:1–25
Liam Goligher
Liam has served as a pastor in Ireland, Canada, London and in his native Scotland. Since 2011, he has been Senior Minister at Tenth Presbyterian Church in Philadelphia, USA. Liam is the author of *Ezekiel*, the 30-day devotional in Keswick Ministries' Food for the Journey series.

1 John 3:10 – 4:21
David Jackman

David is a former president of the Proclamation Trust. He founded the Cornhill Training Course in 1991 and was the minister at Above Bar Church, Southampton, from 1976 to 1991. He is the author of a number of books, including *The Message of John's Letters* in The Bible Speaks Today series.

Revelation 2:1–7
Leith Samuel

Leith was the minister at Above Bar Church, Southampton, from 1953 to 1980, overseeing much change and expansion. Before that, he was an evangelist with Inter-Varsity Fellowship (now UCCF).

Preface

What is the collective name for a group of preachers? A troop, a gaggle, a chatter, a pod . . . ? I'm not sure! But in this Food for the Journey series, we have gathered an excellent group of Bible teachers to help us to unpack the Scriptures and understand some of the core issues that every Christian needs to know.

Each book is based on a particular theme and contains excerpts from messages given by much loved Keswick Convention speakers, past and present. When necessary, the language has been updated, but, on the whole, this is what you would have heard had you been listening in the tent on Skiddaw Street. A wide, though not exhaustive, selection of Bible passages explores the key theme, and each day of the devotional ends with a fresh section on how to apply God's Word to your own life and situation.

Whether you are a Convention regular or have never been to Keswick, this Food for the Journey series provides a unique opportunity to study the Scriptures and a particular topic with a range of gifted Bible teachers by your side. Each book is designed to fit in your jacket pocket or handbag, so that you can read it anywhere – over the breakfast table, on the commute into work or college, while you are waiting in your car, during your lunch break or in bed at night. Wherever life's journey takes you, time in God's Word is vital nourishment for your spiritual journey.

Our prayer is that these devotionals become your daily feast, a nourishing opportunity to meet with God through his Word. Read, meditate on, apply and pray through the Scriptures given for each day, and allow God's truths to take root and transform your life.

If these devotionals whet your appetite for more, there is a 'For further study' section at the end of each book. You can also visit our website <www.keswickministries.org> to find the full range of books, study guides, USB sticks and downloads available.

Let the word of Christ dwell in you richly.
(Colossians 3:16, ESV)

Introduction
Outrageous love

The young couple gazed into each other's eyes as they talked excitedly about their plans for the wedding. They had come to ask my husband, a local church pastor, to marry them. After he asked a few probing questions, they admitted that there was one thing they would like to change: 'For the vows, instead of "for richer, for poorer, in sickness and in health . . . for as long as we both shall live", we want to say "as long as we both shall love".'

They thought they were being romantic, but what were they really promising? To stay together as long as they felt the first flush of romance, as long as they found each other physically attractive or as long as each other's career prospects looked good? They were in danger of exchanging a forever-come-what-may commitment for a lesser as-long-as-it-pleases-me arrangement.

'Love' has become an elastic term; it can mean many different things. But, still, each of us longs to experience love that is more than words or emotions, love that is not deterred by our failings or dependent on our performance.

We yearn for a relentless, forever love and often get derailed looking for it in a spouse, family or friends. God is unrivalled in saying to us: 'I have loved you with an everlasting love' (Jeremiah 31:3).

Such a declaration could come only from God who himself is love (1 John 4:8). Love isn't just what God does; it is who he is. God the Father, Son and Holy Spirit exist in an eternal relationship of love, and the Bible reveals how much this three-in-one God loves us. In the Old Testament, God initiated covenants with his people, pledging his love and calling for their faithful obedience. But they failed to keep their promises. So, in his greatest demonstration of love, God established the New Covenant at Calvary. He sent his Son to die in our place. Jesus' death paid the penalty for our sin and made us right with God: 'See what great love the Father has lavished on us, that we should be called children of God! And that is what we are!' (1 John 3:1). Out of sheer love, God did all that needed to be done to save us. He not only forgave us and adopted us into his family – loving us with the same love he has for his Son – but he also sent his Spirit to renew our hearts so that we could truly love and obey him.

Amazingly, God loves us today with the same boundless love that he demonstrated at Calvary. Like King David, we can say, 'Surely your goodness and love will follow me all the days of my life' (Psalm 23:6). God's enduring love brings us security now and hope for whatever the future holds. It reveals itself in compassion, forgiveness and patience. It disciplines us; it is jealous for our wholehearted devotion and demands our obedience.

'Jesus is the true revelation of what love is and what love does' (Rachel Gilson, *Born Again This Way*, The Good Book Company, 2020, p. 27). He is the standard, the benchmark, for what real love looks like. We are called to love those inside and outside the church – even our enemies – with the same sort of practical, sacrificial and indiscriminate love that Jesus did. This radical love, described concisely in 1 Corinthians 13, marks us out as God-followers and demonstrates to the world the plausibility of the gospel. Only those who have experienced God's outrageous love and have been changed by it can offer it to others. Laying down our lives for other people is not something we can do in our own strength. It is the supernatural outflow of being loved by God.

This thirty-day devotional looks at a selected range of Bible passages to help us to comprehend how much God loves us and how we can love others with his love. The book of Ruth introduces us to the sacrificial commitment of covenant love. Hosea 11 paints a picture of divine love. The Gospel of Matthew exhorts us to love our enemies.

Mark calls us to love God with all our heart, soul, mind and strength. John introduces us to the new standard for love – we are to love other believers like Jesus does. Romans encourages us that nothing – no sin or circumstance – can separate us from God's love. The first letter of John confirms that our love for others is proof that we are saved and Revelation 2 cautions against lukewarm love.

This short book is not a call to do more or be more. It is an invitation to bask in God's love, to appreciate afresh its depth and richness, allowing it to warm your heart and empower your service.

Ruth and Hosea

Ruth

The story is set in the time of the judges; it does not focus on heroic figures such as Samson or Gideon but on Naomi, an ordinary woman who found herself in Moab grieving the loss of her husband and two adult sons. The book traces her transformation from despair to hope because of the selfless love of her daughter-in-law Ruth and her relative Boaz. Ruth was from Moab but she left her home, family and religion to return to Bethlehem with Naomi. She also embraced Naomi's God, signalling that inclusion in God's family is dependent not on place of birth or family heritage but on faith expressed by obedience (Romans 1:5). Ruth's loyalty and love for her mother-in-law reflect God's unfailing love for his people. The book ends with a genealogy naming Ruth as a great-grandmother of King David and an ancestor of Christ – a testimony to how God can use our love and obedience for his sovereign purposes.

Hosea

Hosea was a prophet living in the northern kingdom of Israel who called God's people to repentance for almost forty years. Like Isaiah, Jeremiah and Ezekiel, he lived out his message in a dramatically symbolic fashion. God told him to marry Gomer, a promiscuous woman, love her and take her back when she was unfaithful. Hosea's marriage was a picture of God's unfailing love for his people, who had been unfaithful, worshipping the Canaanite gods and attributing their prosperity to them. Despite their disobedience, God longed for the Israelites to return to him so that he could take them back. The love and intimacy of the covenant relationship God has with his people – then and now – is described graphically throughout the book, not only as a marriage relationship but also as that of a father and child.

Day 1

Read Ruth 1:1–22
Key verses: Ruth 1:16–17

....

> [16] But Ruth replied, 'Don't urge me to leave you or to turn back from you. Where you go I will go, and where you stay I will stay. Your people will be my people and your God my God. [17] Where you die I will die, and there I will be buried. May the LORD deal with me, be it ever so severely, if even death separates you and me.'

What torpedoes love in our culture?

Capitalism, by its endorsement of self-interest, and the media, with their preoccupation with erotic images, have played a part. But the real problem is that, for the past fifty years, we have redefined the meaning of love. It is no longer a sacrificial commitment to another person. Love is now considered to be an intensity of feeling within us. This understanding is what makes Ruth, and the book that bears her name, such a candle in the darkness.

The events took place when the judges ruled: 'In those days Israel had no king; everyone did as they saw fit' (Judges 21:25). Society was utterly individualistic and hedonistic – just as it is today. The book of Ruth, even when it was written, would have been seen as very old fashioned because its message is that love is a sacrificial commitment; a laying down of your life for others. The book is about loyalty, duty and the cost that comes from putting the needs of others before your own. It demonstrates how God achieves his purpose in history through insignificant people who trust him enough to take the risks that sacrificial covenant love demands.

The story begins when Naomi and her family leave Bethlehem during a famine and go to Moab as economic refugees. Both her sons marry Moabite women but, sadly, her husband and sons die within a short period of time. Utterly destitute, Naomi plans to return to Bethlehem. Contrary to all good sense and her own best interest, Ruth, her widowed daughter-in-law, commits herself in love to Naomi. Rather than leave this old woman bereft, Ruth abandons her own country of Moab and her religion, and accompanies Naomi to Judah, the southern Israelite kingdom. In her speech, Ruth deliberately echoes the covenant vow (binding promises) of God to Israel in her own covenant vow to Naomi (Ruth 1:16). She declares her forever, come-what-may commitment to Naomi. This covenant relationship is what real love is about!

If Ruth had been interested only in self-fulfilment, she would have abandoned Naomi and gone in search of a husband among her own people. But she is determined to put loyalty to Naomi and Naomi's God first, whatever the sacrifice. Strikingly, Orpah, Naomi's other daughter-in-law, can't face such a cost and she returns to Moab. So two destitute widows, one a Moabite (considered an enemy of Israel), are heading straight for Bethlehem.

Ruth's sacrificial love for Naomi is a pale reflection of God's love and faithfulness to you. God has declared his forever, come-what-may commitment at the cross. There is nothing you can do to make God love you any more and no sin you can commit that would make him love you any less. Jesus laid down his life to save you – that is how loved you are!

Day 2

Read Ruth 3:1–18
Key verses: Ruth 3:8–9

....

> [8]*In the middle of the night something startled the man; he turned – and there was a woman lying at his feet!*
>
>   [9]*'Who are you?' he asked.*
>
>   *'I am your servant Ruth,' she said. 'Spread the corner of your garment over me, since you are a guardian-redeemer of our family.'*

It wouldn't rank very highly as a conventional (or romantic) marriage proposal.

Ruth had arrived in Bethlehem during harvest time and started gleaning in the fields to support herself and Naomi, which is what the homeless and the beggars did. She just happens to go to a field belonging to Boaz (2:3), who just happens to be a member of Naomi's family (2:20).

In the middle of the night, when the party to celebrate the harvest is over, Boaz wakes from sleep on the threshing floor to discover Ruth lying at his feet (3:8). She says to him, 'Spread the corner of your garment over me' (3:9), which means in essence, 'Marry me!'

When Boaz first met Ruth, he was moved by her kindness to Naomi and prayed, 'May you be richly rewarded by the LORD, the God of Israel, under whose wings you have come to take refuge' (2:12). Ruth is now saying, 'Just as you prayed that for me, Boaz, let me come under the protection of God's wings by coming under the protection of your garment!' The word translated 'corner of your garment' is the same word for 'wing'. In Ezekiel, God's spreading of the corner of his garment (that is, 'wing') is used of God when he makes a covenant with his people. Ruth is asking Boaz to be the answer to his own prayers. She's saying, 'Boaz, marry me, and please take care of my mother-in-law. I will not break my covenant and vows of love to her.'

Ruth's covenantal love and kindness to Naomi has impressed Boaz (3:10) but, more importantly, it transforms Naomi. This woman of faith has been devastated family bereavements. She articulates the honest complaint of many believers who find themselves the innocent victims of God's judgment in a fallen world: 'The Lord has afflicted me' (1:21). But Naomi discovers that her cynicism is misplaced and she ends this story with her grandson, Ruth and Boaz's son, in her arms (4:16). What a joy!

How was Naomi's faith restored? By personally experiencing the human love and sacrificial service of Ruth. Her faith in the covenant love of God was restored because another human being demonstrated such love to her. The kindness of God was real to Naomi because of the kindness of Ruth.

Have you come under the Redeemer's wing? Are you sheltering under the corner of his garment? If so, you are absolutely secure in God's covenant love in Christ. Today, thank him for the love he has lavished on you and consider to whom you will show that same covenant love. God calls us to love others with the love he has shown us. So who is your Naomi? What task has God asked you to do that will require you to lay down your life for the sake of others?

Day 3

Read Ruth 4:1–22
Key verses: Ruth 4:5–6

....

> 5 Then Boaz said, 'On the day you buy the land from Naomi, you also acquire Ruth the Moabite, the dead man's widow, in order to maintain the name of the dead with his property.'
>
> 6 At this, the guardian-redeemer said, 'Then I cannot redeem it because I might endanger my own estate. You redeem it yourself. I cannot do it.'

What would you do for love?

Boaz is depicted as a servant-hearted, godly, self-sacrificing believer. He bore Ruth no resentment when she gleaned in his fields (2:8); he told his men not to harm her (2:9); he acknowledged and encouraged her godliness (2:12); and he sent her home with food (2:17). Naomi actually tells us that Boaz is famed for his kindness (2:20).

And now, just as Ruth was contrasted with her sister-in-law in chapter 1, Boaz is contrasted with another relative. This unnamed man wants the land that Naomi's husband, Elimelech, left when he went to Moab. He has first refusal and says that he will buy it. He ultimately shies away from covenant love, however, when he realizes that he'll have to support Ruth and Naomi, as well as provide an heir for Elimelech's family.

His excuse: 'I might endanger my own estate!' Never mind his duty to God's law or his responsibility to care for Elimelech's family, this man wants the land but not the widows. The same reasoning stops us caring. We think, 'I can't risk this sort of sacrifice and self-giving. What about me, what about my resources and what about my own boundaries?' This man walks away from Naomi and, in doing so, walks away from his duty, his calling. But Boaz does the right thing. He buys the field and takes on the care of Ruth and Naomi, too.

The big picture is that covenant love is going to put Boaz and Ruth right into the middle of salvation history. Their child Obed was the grandfather of David, whose descendent was Christ (4:17)! But Boaz and Ruth couldn't see how God was sovereignly working his purposes out. All they could see was Naomi and the call to obedience and covenant love.

This story is designed to deprogramme us from our selfish, individualistic, therapeutic attitudes towards love, a love that is about an intensity of feeling, rather than a sacrificial commitment to another person. The message was needed in the time of the judges and it is needed today. It's a story that is meant to encourage us; if we really want to know what love means, in its fullest and richest form, then we must be willing for commitment and sacrifice as the price of love, for we live in the shadow of Calvary.

Many times each day we face a choice: to be like the unnamed relative and preserve our resources and boundaries or be like Boaz and love sacrificially. Such love is costly, especially when our circumstances are difficult and God's purposes are hidden. But we mustn't stop loving. We must keep on laying down our lives. Our obedience reflects God's love, delights his heart and is being used by him in ways we could never imagine to work out his sovereign plan.

Day 4

Read Hosea 10:1 – 11:11

Key verses: Hosea 11:1–2

· ·

> [1] *When Israel was a child, I loved him,*
>   *and out of Egypt I called my son.*
> [2] *But the more they were called,*
>   *the more they went away from me.*
> *They sacrificed to the Baals*
>   *and they burned incense to images.*

Most parents capture those early memories of a baby's first steps or first spoonful of solid food. In Hosea 10 – 11, it's as if God were taking out his photo album and poignantly remembering how Israel used to be before its fall from grace. He gives three snapshots, each designed to remind Israel of the great start it had in life.

• *The fruitful vine (10:1–8).* God has planted and taken great care of the vineyard and the vine is heavy with luscious, ripe grapes. But, perversely, instead of giving God glory for all the prosperity that he has showered upon them, the Israelites turn from him and worship other gods. In fact, the more God blesses them, the more they praise the Baals, the fertility gods of the Canaanites, as if the Baals had provided their prosperity.

- *A prize cow (10:9–15)*. This young cow is well-trained, in prime condition and already loves to thresh (verse 11). God, as it were, brings this cow home, places a yoke upon her neck and starts her ploughing. The picture speaks of the early promise of Israel, chosen by God to do his work (verse 12). But instead of being willing to be used in God's service, growing the crop of holiness, Israel plants wickedness and reaps evil (verse 13). Such promise ends in tragedy.

- *A beloved child (11:1–11)*. The images have steadily become more intimate. We've moved from horticulture to the farmyard, and now we're in the family. The child, Israel, is so precious in the sight of God. God redeemed Israel out of slavery in Egypt to be his son. However, the fatherhood of God is not presented here to comfort Israel but to confront her with the awfulness of her sin (verse 2).

To underline the full horror of what they're doing, God takes out of the album a photograph that every parent treasures: an infant taking his first steps (verse 3). The child falls and hurts his knee; Dad picks him up and kisses it better. God says, 'I did that for you. You don't realize it was I who healed you.' The final photograph is of the child in his high chair. Dad is leaning down, feeding him and beaming again with pride and devotion (verse 4). It's a picture of divine love. And yet it's a love that has been spurned. We tend to think of sin in impersonal terms – as breaking certain laws and standards – but God, through Hosea, reminds us that sin is intensely personal. When Christians sin, we are spurning our divine Father. Sin is serious. It matters.

Your sin is not just a harmless outburst of anger or bout of selfishness; it's not just a quick glance at a web page or idle gossip. It's a spurning of God's love. Today, in your fight to resist sin, meditate on the immense privileges that you have: God has blessed you abundantly, chosen you to serve him and adopted you into his family. You are able to call the living God 'my Father'. You are precious to him.

Day 5

Read Hosea 10:1 – 11:11
Key verse: Hosea 11:8

. . . .

> [8]*How can I give you up, Ephraim?*
>   *How can I hand you over, Israel?*
> *How can I treat you like Admah?*
>   *How can I make you like Zeboyim?*
> *My heart is changed within me;*
>   *all my compassion is aroused.*

Do you really believe that God loves you?

We know how wicked we've been and the judgment we deserve, so believing that God loves us is often a hard truth to accept.

The book of Hosea is dominated by the themes of sin and judgment, and that message is underlined by powerful pictures of God as husband and father. Just like Hosea, who takes Gomer back, despite all that she has done,

God can't switch off his love for his bride or, to use the image of chapter 11, his love for his child.

God is all churned up inside. On the one hand, he must judge the people (10:2, 13; 11:5). He made it clear before they entered the land that if they disobeyed him, they would be evicted. But on the other hand, he can't abandon them. Before they entered the land, God had promised Abraham: 'I will make you into a great nation, and I will bless you . . . all peoples on earth will be blessed through you' (Genesis 12:2–3). This is the great tension throughout the Old Testament. How can God meet the demands of his justice and, at the same time, the demands of his love? How can God be faithful to his covenant promises of love and remain just at the same time?

That tension is finally resolved only in Christ. Judgment came in 722 BC, when the Assyrians destroyed the nation of Israel. But that was not the end. Seven hundred years later, a baby boy was born in Bethlehem and taken by his parents to Egypt to protect him from Herod. Then he returned; Matthew quotes Hosea 11:1, 'And so was fulfilled what the Lord had said through the prophet: "Out of Egypt I called my son"' (Matthew 2:15). You see, Israel had blown it. They'd disobeyed God. They had to face his judgment. But then came the Lord Jesus Christ.

He was the 'true vine' (John 15:1). He was Israel as Israel should have been, the perfect son of God who always lived in obedience to his Father. Therefore, he didn't deserve to face the judgment that came upon Old Testament Israel. Yet willingly, in his infinite mercy and grace, he took the judgment that God's people deserved so that all who trust in him can become like Israel: God's son; forgiven and blessed.

The lion is roaring lovingly (Hosea 11:10), calling us back from Egypt, Assyria and wherever the nation has been scattered. Christ is inviting all people, Jews and Gentiles, to join God's Israel, his holy people, that we might know God as our Father. The exile is over and he's calling us back home.

Today, praise God that, because Jesus was the perfect Son, we can know God as Father. His obedience on the cross means that God does not look on us in judgment and anger but says, 'I love you; I sent my Son to die for you. You can call me "Father". I forgive you; I accept you. Come home.'

Matthew and Mark

Matthew

Matthew was one of the twelve disciples. He left his work as a tax collector to follow Jesus. His knowledge of Jewish customs, extensive quotations from the Old Testament and emphasis on Jesus' descent from King David seem to indicate that he wrote his Gospel account primarily for Jewish believers. His aim was to confirm that Jesus is the Messiah and the fulfilment of Old Testament prophecies. His Gospel is arranged around five discourses, the most famous of which, the Sermon on the Mount (chapters 5 – 7), includes Jesus' radical call to be like God by loving our enemies.

Mark

This Gospel was written by the young man who abandoned Paul on his first mission trip. Barnabas wanted to give Mark a second chance and invite him to accompany them on the next journey, but Paul refused and, ultimately, Paul and Barnabas parted ways. Thankfully, over time, Mark proved his commitment to Christ and he and Paul were fully reconciled (2 Timothy 4:11). Mark based his Gospel on Peter's preaching and it is a fast-paced, easy-to-read account of Jesus' ministry. It was most probably written for the Gentile believers in Rome who were facing the Emperor Nero's persecution. Mark encourages them to persevere by highlighting themes of suffering, discipleship and the cross. He records Jesus' teaching on the greatest commandment and the kind of love that God requires.

Day 6

Read Matthew 5:43–48
Key verses: Matthew 5:43–44

....

> [43] *You have heard that it was said, 'Love your neighbour and hate your enemy.'* [44] *But I tell you, love your enemies and pray for those who persecute you.*

'Love your enemies' is a phrase known by people who would never darken the door of a church. It is one of the most quoted sayings of the early church and at the very heart of the Sermon on the Mount. At the core of the Christian ethic, we are called to love people as God loves them, without discrimination.

This call to love enemies is difficult to hear. Around the world believers are tortured and even killed for their faith. Many Christians have been wounded by toxic church battles and have faced discrimination in the workplace, and some are experiencing domestic abuse.* Loving enemies was no easier for first-century believers who lived with the brutal reality of Roman occupation.

Jesus' words were in stark contrast to the 'love your neighbour and hate your enemy' maxim invented by religious leaders to ease the burden of the law. The legal retribution of 'an eye for an eye' was transformed by Jesus' new initiative: 'do not resist an evil person' (see Matthew 5:38–42). If you're taken to court unjustly by someone who wants to shame you and he takes your coat, give him your shirt as well. As you stand almost naked, you will not be the shamed one, that person will be. If you meet a Roman soldier, who by law, was allowed to make you carry his backpack for a mile, carry it a second mile. This will leave the Roman soldier, one of the hated enemies, totally amazed.

How can anyone obey this seemingly impossible command? When Jesus tells us to 'love' our enemies he uses the word *agape*. There are other Greek words that imply there is something attractive or desirable in the object of love, but to have *agape* is to love without reason. It is the

---

* Please understand that you are not required to remain in a dangerous home environment. If reading these verses causes you distress or confusion, seek the support of a trusted group of Christian friends to help you to understand how these verses might relate to you personally.

love that can be born only by the power of the Holy Spirit. C. S. Lewis says that we shouldn't spend time pondering whether we love an enemy, we should behave as if we do, so that we 'will presently come to love him' (*Mere Christianity*, Collins, 2012, p. 131). That's what Jesus is saying. He knew that love could begin only when we pray for an enemy. Prayer is the action that moves the will. Don't wait to feel love in your heart; pray for God's power to bless a persecutor and forgive an enemy.

'When [God] tells us to love our enemies he gives, along with the command, the love itself.'
(Corrie ten Boom, a prisoner at Ravensbrück concentration camp, from *The Hiding Place*, Hodder & Stoughton, 2004, p. 221)

Day 7

Read Matthew 5:43–48
Key verses: Matthew 5:44–47

....

> *44But I tell you, love your enemies and pray for those who persecute you, 45that you may be children of your Father in heaven. He causes his sun to rise on the evil and the good, and sends rain on the righteous and the unrighteous. 46If you love those who love you, what reward will you get? Are not even the tax collectors doing that? 47And if you greet only your own people, what are you doing more than others? Do not even pagans do that?*

Why should we love our enemies? Because it's Godlike.

We prove that we're children of our heavenly Father by displaying the family likeness. God loves without discrimination, and when we love like this, we share his character. He sends rain on evil people and good people, on the righteous and unrighteous. God is generous even to the morally undeserving. His sun and rain are a sign of his common grace, and they are intended to draw people to his saving grace in Jesus Christ.

Your own story proves that God loves without discrimination. While you were God's enemy, he died for you. He cleansed you of your sins, adopted you into his family and commissioned you to be an ambassador of the good news. Each follower of Jesus, saved by grace, is a living testimony that an enemy can be transformed into a friend and become part of God's family.

But Jesus doesn't stop there. We are to love our enemies, not just because it's Godlike but also because we are called to a life of 'more than' (verse 47). Jesus asks, 'What are you doing *more than* tax collectors who love their friends?' His point is that even cheats and swindlers have friends. They enjoy loving relationships, good marriages and are generous with their money. Jesus is saying, 'I want "more than" in my disciples.' There is nothing exceptional about loving your own kind and greeting your own friends. What is exceptional is loving your enemy and praying for those who persecute you. The world is crying out for examples of that kind of discipleship.

Is the way you love demonstrably different from your non-Christian friends? Are you living a 'more than' kind of life? This may mean:

- forgiving a Christian who has hurt you;
- praying and doing good to family members or work colleagues who ridicule your faith;
- finding ways to serve and share the gospel with people in your city who have backgrounds different from yours;
- intentionally praying for political and social groups that have an anti-Christian agenda;
- showing hospitality in your home and befriending those in church who are not 'your own people';
- being kind and respectful on social media to those who disagree with you.

Pray for God's help to share his character and live a 'more than' kind of life that draws Christians and non-Christians to him.

Day 8

Read Matthew 5:43–48
Key verses: Matthew 5:43–44, 48

. . . .

> [43] *You have heard that it was said, 'Love your neighbour and hate your enemy.'* [44] *But I tell you, love your enemies and pray for those who persecute you,* [45] *that you may be children of your Father in heaven . . .* [48] *Be perfect, therefore, as your heavenly Father is perfect.*

When our feelings have been hurt, the urge to get even is powerful and, in the spirit of retaliation, almost anything is excused in our culture. But God calls us to live radically different lives.

We are to love our enemies because we are called to be perfect (see Day 7 for the other reasons Jesus gives for loving our enemies). Jesus doesn't mean perfect in the sense of sinless perfection. According to the Sermon on the Mount, we can't have perfect lives without sin on earth. How could we if Jesus taught us to pray in the

Lord's Prayer 'forgive us our debts [sins]' (Matthew 6:12; see Luke 11:4)?

Perfection, total life with God, will be ours in the new heaven and the new earth. Meanwhile, the command to be perfect is a call to maturity, to completeness and to wholeness. It means a life entirely at one with the will of God – a longing to fulfil the family likeness and reflect it in our living; a desire to love without discrimination.

How can we be perfect like this? How can we love our enemies and pray for those who persecute us? We look to Jesus on the cross, who, when he was mocked by his enemies, didn't retaliate. When his enemies beat him, he took the pain. When his enemies nailed him to the cross, he prayed for them: 'Father, forgive them, for they do not know what they are doing' (Luke 23:34). After Jesus died, the people on Golgotha, who had come to witness the crucifixion, 'beat their breasts and went away' (Luke 23:48). Would they have done this if Jesus hadn't prayed for them? Was it not this prayer for the enemy that distressed them? He could have cursed them. He could have threatened them. He could have called down his judgment on them. But he prayed for his enemies.

What is God's will for my life? In Matthew 5, God makes his will clear and it is a comprehensive, for-all-time command. Like God, we are to be perfect, reflecting his likeness by loving our enemies and praying for those who persecute us. In the light of this, whom do you need to love and pray for today? Draw strength and encouragement from the example of Christ on the cross. 'In your relationships with one another, have the same mindset as Christ Jesus' (Philippians 2:5).

Day 9

Read Mark 12:28–34
Key verse: Mark 12:28

....

> 28*One of the teachers of the law came and heard them debating. Noticing that Jesus had given them a good answer, he asked him, 'Of all the commandments, which is the most important?'*

You would be forgiven for thinking that this was a simple question.

In fact, it was a massive contemporary debate. The Jewish rabbis had identified 613 commands in the Torah, the first five books of the Old Testament. The Mishnah, the written collection of the Jewish oral tradition, says that charity and deeds of kindness outweigh all the other commandments. Midrash (Jewish commentary) on the book of Haggai concludes that purity and temple service – sacrifices, rituals and offerings – are what count as Torah.

What does Jesus reply? He cites the Shema (Deuteronomy 6:4–5). Every good Jew prayed the Shema every day, 'Love the LORD your God with all your heart and with all your soul and with all your strength,' but Jesus adds, 'Love your neighbour as yourself,' a statement from Leviticus 19:18 encapsulating a whole list of laws. Jesus' summary of the whole law is love God; love neighbour.

Moses received the Ten Commandments on two tablets. The first tablet was concerned with a right relationship with God – don't make idols, don't blaspheme, observe the Sabbath. Tablet two was about right treatment of your neighbour: not murdering, stealing, coveting, lying or committing adultery. In Mark 12, Jesus is saying, 'Here's a summary of the two tablets. Tablet one: love God; tablet two: love your neighbour. They are inextricably and intrinsically bound together.' If you love God but fail to care for your neighbour, you don't really love God at all. If you love your neighbour and do acts of philanthropy and kindness but don't have a relationship with God, you're not loving your neighbour properly either.

In his magnum opus, *The City of God*, Augustine, a fifth-century North African bishop, asked, 'Is it OK to love yourself? Is it Christian?' You can't help loving yourself because it is natural simply to seek your own highest well-being, goodness, joy, satisfaction and happiness. Augustine concluded it was a good thing but added that you find the greatest satisfaction and your highest well-being as a creature in relationship to your Creator. So to love your neighbour as yourself means to seek the same thing for him or her. Augustine argued that you can't separate these two commands. You can't be a pious individual who hates your neighbour because you're not really loving God. And you can't love your neighbour without helping that person to find reconciliation with his or her Maker. You don't really love your neighbour if you don't love God.

'Which is the most important commandment?' Jesus' answer is that it's love. Having love for God and love for your neighbour is the way you fulfil the law.

Does your behaviour reflect the fact that love is the most important commandment? We believe God and we serve him, but do we really love him? At work or at home, are we known for our love? Without love, we accomplish nothing (see 1 Corinthians 13:1–3). Today, take time to delight in God, valuing him above all else and, in your interactions with others, make love the priority.

Day 10

Read Mark 12:28–34
Key verse: Mark 12:30

....

³⁰*Love the Lord your God with all your heart and with all your soul and with all your mind and with all your strength.*

Do you love God with all your heart and soul?

I suspect that our culture's understanding of the heart and the Bible's understanding are different things. When the Bible uses the word 'heart', it's not talking about our emotions, moods or the tingly feeling that occurs when boy meets girl. In the Bible, the heart is the seat of the will; it's the decision-making centre. It's not a *feeling* towards something or someone; it's a *decision* towards something or someone. It's an act of the will with regard to the other person.

This is significant because if love were just a feeling, it would come and go. Jesus is saying that to love the Lord with all your heart is a *decision*. That means you don't just go to church when you feel like going to church. You don't just keep up your personal devotions when you're in the mood and you feel close to God. No. You *decide* that you will love God through thick and thin, not just when it feels good. Our culture says feelings lead to actions and, in some cases, that's true. The Bible says it's the other way round – we have to decide to love God and then the feelings and the emotions follow.

The second thing Jesus says is that you must 'love the Lord your God with all your soul'. In the Hebrew of Deuteronomy 6, the word *nephesh*, translated 'soul', actually means 'life'; it doesn't mean 'soul' at all. 'Soul' is not a particularly helpful translation for Western twenty-first-century people because we think of something immaterial and ghostly. We have this strict division between body and soul. Hebrew thought doesn't have that, so when it says, 'Love your God with all your *nephesh*', it means love God with all your life, with every fibre of your being and existence, every moment of every day. Nothing is off-limits to God. There's no part of your life that you can rope off, put a 'no entry' sign over and say, 'God, I love you but you just can't come here. Don't challenge me on this. It's private property.' To love God with all your soul means with every part of you; every bit of your life and existence is God's property and is for his glory.

Is there a relationship, hobby or possession that you have made 'off-limits' to God? Heed the Spirit's call and, in his strength, surrender this area of your life to God. But don't stop there. Loving God with all your heart and soul is not about a spectacular, one-off display of obedience but daily surrender in the routine of life, over years and decades – it is a 'long obedience in the same direction' (see Eugene Peterson, *Long Obedience in the Same Direction*, IVP, 2021). Pray: 'God, I want nothing to be off-limits to you. Whatever comes across my path today, help me to love you with all that I am and with all that I have. For your glory. Amen.'

Day 11

Read Mark 12:28–34
Key verse: Mark 12:30

....

30 Love the Lord your God with all your heart and with all your soul and with all your mind and with all your strength.

Are you loving God with all your mind and strength?

Interestingly, 'mind' isn't mentioned in Deuteronomy 6:5. The Hebrew of Deuteronomy 6 calls us to love God with all our heart, soul and strength. In the Greek translations of the Hebrew, you get a couple of variations in the translation of the last word, 'strength': some say 'strength' and others, 'mind'. I think Jesus is saying that both these traditions capture something of the essence of Deuteronomy 6, which is why I presume he pulls them together and turns the command into a fourfold, instead of a threefold, one.

Loving God with your mind isn't theological study for study's sake, it's about getting to know a person. You can't love someone you don't have a personal relationship with. In the Bible, knowledge is never an abstract, cognitive thing. The Hebrew verb for 'know' connotes the intimate personal knowledge between a man and a wife. If you want to love God, you have to grow in your knowledge of him, which means daily reading, studying and meditating on the Bible.

The final element of this fourfold command is 'love the Lord your God . . . with all your strength'. Love God with all your power and energy. Love is not a feeling; it's an action. It's a verb. The Targum is the Jewish translation of the Hebrew Scriptures into the lingua franca of the day, which was Aramaic. It's fascinating that the Targum translates the word 'strength' in Deuteronomy 6 into the Aramaic word *mamona*: mammon – money or possessions. Jewish scholars looked at this word 'strength' and understood it to mean not so much physical strength and energy as resources.

The command is to 'love the Lord your God with all your heart . . . with all your soul . . . with all your mind and with all your *stuff*': to love God not only with every fibre of your existence but also with everything he has given you. Everything we have is a gift from God to be richly enjoyed and that includes loving God with our *things* – our possessions, time, talents and treasures.

The way we study the Bible, open our homes, share our meals, spend our money and use our time reveal the depth of our love for God. Most of us need to release our grasp on what we have, remembering that it is God's 'stuff', not ours, as Randy Alcorn discovered:

> If God was the owner, I was the manager. I needed to adopt a steward's mentality toward the assets He had entrusted – not given – to me. A steward manages assets for the owner's benefit. The steward carries no sense of entitlement to the assets he manages. It's his job to find out what the owner wants done with his assets, then carry out his will.
>
> (Randy Alcorn, *The Treasure Principle*, Multnomah, 2017, p. 26)

Day 12

Read Mark 12:28–34
Key verses: Mark 12:29–31

....

29'*The most important [commandment],*' *answered Jesus, 'is this: "Hear, O Israel: the Lord our God, the Lord is one.* 30*Love the Lord your God with all your heart and with all your soul and with all your mind and with all your strength."* 31*The second is this: "Love your neighbour as yourself." There is no commandment greater than these.'*

What is the relationship between loving God and loving your neighbour?

In the Promised Land, Moses taught the people to observe God's laws carefully:

For this will show your wisdom and understanding to the nations, who will hear about all these decrees and say, 'Surely this great nation is a wise and understanding people.' What other nation is so great as to have their

gods near them the way the Lord our God is near us when-
ever we pray to him? And what other nation is so great as
to have such righteous decrees and laws as this body of
laws I am setting before you today?
(Deuteronomy 4:6–8)

Moses is saying to the Israelites, 'If you obey this law,
then the nations will see something about your lives, your
ethics, your love for God, and it will captivate, compel
and convict them.'

This idea in Deuteronomy 4 and Mark 12 is that our love
for God is itself a witness. There is something proclamatory
about our lives lived in front of neighbours, colleagues,
unbelieving family and a watching community. And our
witness is not just as individuals but also as a church when
we feed the poor, provide debt counselling and get
involved with groups for abused women or those struggling with addiction. As we love a community, they see
something of a love for God and a love for neighbour,
and it captivates them.

Lesslie Newbigin, a well-known writer on mission in the
twentieth century, described the church as the plausibility
structure for the gospel. If you say, 'God loves you,' and
you don't live it out, you undermine the message. But
church members who genuinely love God, one another

and their community provide a plausibility structure for the message of a God who loves a broken world.

This is profoundly challenging. We say we want our churches to grow and people to become Christians but, at the same time, we want church to stay the same, be a size in which we all know one another. We profess to love the world but, truthfully, we like life to remain small, safe, secure and personal, and we'd rather our churches were like members' clubs. But that's not the raison d'être of the church; that's not why we're still here. We are here because there's a world in desperate need of the grace and love of God.

> The primary reality of which we have to take account in seeking for a Christian impact on public life is the Christian congregation. How is it possible that the gospel should be credible, that people should come to believe that the power which has the last word in human affairs is represented by a man hanging on a cross? . . . The only answer, the only hermeneutic of the gospel, is a congregation of men and women who believe it and live by it.
>
> (Lesslie Newbigin, quoted in Michael W. Goheen, *The Church and Its Vocation*, Baker Academic, 2018, p. 81)

Day 13

Read Mark 12:28–34
Key verses: Mark 12:32–34

• •

³²*'Well said, teacher,' the man replied. 'You are right in saying that God is one and there is no other but him.* ³³*To love him with all your heart, with all your understanding and with all your strength, and to love your neighbour as yourself is more important than all burnt offerings and sacrifices.'*

³⁴*When Jesus saw that he had answered wisely, he said to him, 'You are not far from the kingdom of God.' And from then on no one dared ask him any more questions.*

Can you feel the tension?

The religious leaders are looking for a way to arrest and kill Jesus (Mark 12:12), so they ask him questions in the temple to try to catch him out. Up to this point, Jesus' answers rebuke the rabbis but this one ends with a commendation. The man speaking understands that faith and grace lead to actions, and that a real relationship with God is more important than burnt offerings. So Jesus replies, 'You are not far from the kingdom of God.' There is a word of commendation for this religious leader, but it's also a bit of a slap.

This man would have studied for thirty years to be a rabbi. He knows his Bible far better than we do; he's probably got students of his own. And Jesus says, 'You're not far from the kingdom.' Can you imagine the crowd's response? If this guy can't get in, what hope is there for any of us? In some ways, that's the point. This greatest commandment should drive us to our knees as we realize how far we fall short of God's holy standards. God's standard of perfection – to love him with all our heart, soul, mind and strength and love our neighbours as ourselves – leaves us nothing to say but 'Lord, forgive me, I'm a great sinner in need of a great saviour'.

Where can we find forgiveness? Jesus. He is the only man who has ever kept the greatest commandment perfectly. He is the only one who has ever truly loved God his Father with all his heart, soul, mind and strength. He's the only one who has ever truly loved his neighbours as himself, laying down his life for them. Jesus lived the life that we should live but can't, and died the death that we deserve so that we can find forgiveness and reconciliation. He is the sacrificial substitute. He takes my sin and credits me with his perfect record of righteousness: the great divine exchange.

Does Jesus' death nullify the law? Jeremiah 31:33 says it's written on the heart. My obedience to the law now is not (and never was) to earn favour; it's a response to grace, to all that Jesus has done for me. God gives me his Holy Spirit and he writes his law on my heart, enabling me to live a life that, not perfectly but truly, shows love for God and neighbour.

Jesus is indeed a great and all-sufficient Saviour. He forgives our sin, gives us his righteousness and makes it possible to live a life of love. Hallelujah! What a Saviour!

John

John, 'the disciple whom Jesus loved' (13:23), wrote this Gospel. The purpose of this eyewitness testimony of Jesus' life and ministry is to help us to 'believe that Jesus is the Messiah, the Son of God, and that by believing [we] may have life in his name' (20:31). Chapters 12 – 19 focus exclusively on Jesus' last week – the Last Supper, his final teaching, his prayers for his disciples and all believers, as well as his trial and crucifixion. The key theme of the book is stated in 3:16: 'For God so loved the world that he gave his one and only Son, that whoever believes in him shall not perish but have eternal life.' John explains that this Calvary love is the benchmark for how God's people must love one another and display his love to the world.

Day 14

Read John 13:1–38
Key verses: John 13:34–35

• •

> [34] *A new command I give you: love one another. As I have loved you, so you must love one another.* [35] *By this everyone will know that you are my disciples, if you love one another.*

Final instructions are important.

Jesus' last command, recorded in John 13:34–35, leaves us in no doubt about the priority of love. He makes it clear that love is imperative, innovative and internal.

• *Imperative*. 'Love one another' is not a word of advice or wishful thinking; it is a command. But can an emotion really be commanded? The Bible continually commands us to love (Deuteronomy 6:5; Matthew 22:37) because, in Scripture, an emotion is not an instinctive reaction that you can't control, shape or discipline. According to the Bible, emotions are an indication of what we truly believe and value. As Christians, we love things that are good rather than things that are worthless. So Scripture can command us to love because love isn't just an unbridled, instinctive emotion; it is an aspect of our being that is linked to knowledge and that leads to action which we can consecrate to Christ. It's when we surrender our emotions that we begin to feel true affection for God.

• *Innovative*. Leviticus 19:18 tells us to love our neighbour. So why does Jesus say that this is a new command? It is simply because he sets a new standard. We are to love one another not, in the Old Covenant way, as ourselves but, rather, as Jesus says to his disciples, 'As I have loved you.' Jesus is about to go to the cross, and this new commandment exhorts us not to love partially but as Jesus has loved us. The cross and resurrection will bring in a new era in God's salvation plan. Soon, Jesus will ascend, the Holy Spirit will be given and the age of the church will be launched. The old command is being repeated and intensified for the New Covenant era.

• *Internal*. Elsewhere in the Bible we are told to love the world but, on this occasion, Jesus tells us to love those in the church. Sometimes it's easier to love the world than it is to love a fellow church member. The church is a diverse mix of ages, ethnicities, educational back-grounds, emotional intelligence and physical abilities. Our love is not optional or reserved for those who are like us. We cannot choose whom we want to love. We are to love without qualification.

William Temple, who was the Archbishop of Canterbury from 1942 to 1944, pointed out that this simple command is actually impossible. We don't have it within us. But then he added: 'Except so far as we are in Christ. He himself will make it possible for us' (William Temple, *Readings in St John's Gospel*, Macmillan, 1961, p. 215). Christ is inviting us to be a channel of his supernatural grace, flowing through us, into the lives of other people.

Heavenly Father, thank you that obedience is possible. Thank you that, because we belong to Christ and draw on his power, we can love other believers as he does – without reservation and without qualification. Help us to surrender our emotions to you and become channels of your grace, blessing the lives of others today. Amen.

Day 15

Read John 13:1–38
Key verses: John 13:34–35

....

³⁴A new command I give you: love one another. As I have loved you, so you must love one another. ³⁵By this everyone will know that you are my disciples, if you love one another.

Whom do you measure yourself against?

When it comes to love, the person we are to compare ourselves to is Jesus. We are to love as he has loved. Jesus loved practically, selflessly, patiently and sacrificially.

- *Practically*. The same night Jesus gave this command to his disciples, he took off his outer garments, picked up a basin and a towel and washed their feet (John 13:3–5). His love was down to earth, with 'sleeves rolled up'; it was practical.

- *Selflessly*. Jesus didn't love just when it suited him but when he was caught off guard and at inconvenient moments. Think of the occasions when he slipped away from the crowds to get some rest and they followed him. He ministered to them and did some of his greatest miracles even in those trying circumstances. Or think of the times when he appeared to be focused on one agenda. Remember the Canaanite woman who asked for help (Matthew 15:21–28)? Jesus said he wasn't there for her; he'd come for the Israelites, but her persistent faith led him to change his agenda and serve her. We can slip into the professional 'I'll care' mode: the 'I'll love when I'm on duty, when I'm the Christian leader or when I'm working' mode. But Jesus loved selflessly.

- *Patiently*. John 13 begins:

    It was just before the Passover Festival. Jesus knew that the hour had come for him to leave this world and go to the Father. Having loved his own who were in the world, he loved them *to the end*.
    (verse 1, emphasis added)

Likewise, Paul says that Christians are to be patient, 'bearing with one another in love . . . [and to] be kind and compassionate to one another, forgiving each other, just as in Christ God forgave you' (Ephesians 4:2, 32). We often judge people by standards that we don't apply to ourselves. Instead, we need to put ourselves in the other person's position and not give up loving too deeply or too soon.

- *Sacrificially*. The command comes as Jesus talks about his being 'glorified'. That's a code word in John's Gospel for being lifted up on the cross as if it were his coronation throne. Stripped of his clothes, battered, bruised and denied his human rights, Jesus is to be crucified. This was his moment of glorification. Like Jesus, we are called upon to love sacrificially – to open up our homes when it's inconvenient, to be available when we're tired, to spend money, time and self, laying down our lives for others.

That's what it takes to love as Jesus loved us.

> See how he loved him!
> (John 11:36)

The Jewish leaders' comment on how much Jesus loved Lazarus could apply to each one of us. We are so loved! Reflect on the infinite scope of God's love in Christ: the practical evidence of his daily care, his patience in forgiving our sins, his relentless compassion when we are weak and, most of all, his sacrificial death to save us.

Today, thank God for his love for you and ask for help to love like Jesus.

Day 16

Read John 13:1–38
Key verses: John 13:34–35

....

³⁴*A new command I give you: love one another. As I have loved you, so you must love one another.* ³⁵*By this everyone will know that you are my disciples, if you love one another.*

What about loving the world?

Surely, we should look to do mission, not just maintenance ministry; we should be outward-looking rather than staying in our 'holy huddle', shouldn't we?

Yes! But unless we love those inside the church, we undermine the gospel message by the way we behave and relate to one another. Francis Schaeffer said that love is the 'final apologetic', the ultimate argument for the gospel (*The Mark of the Christian*, IVP, 1971, p. 13). Jesus has commissioned us to share the gospel, but if we talk without loving in true, practical, down-to-earth ways, then we'll never engage in convincing mission. The early Christians were known by their love. The ancient Father of the Church, Tertullian, was able to write to his critics and say, '"See," they [those outside the church] say, "how these Christians love one another" (for they themselves hate one another); "and how they are ready to die for each other" (for they themselves are readier to kill each other)' (*Apologeticus*, ch. 39, sect. 7).

Jesus calls us to love not only because it's the final apologetic but also because it demonstrates the family likeness. Jesus says, 'If you love like this, everyone will know that you are *my* disciples.' This is how you'd expect the disciples of Jesus to live and behave. They wear the family uniform. The tragedy is that, so often, we wear a different uniform. In the name of Christ, we have incited people to hatred and violence, and we have engaged in false nationalism.

What about you? Do you love those in your church or have you been the cause of dissension and unhappiness? Are there people you've been avoiding? If you feel loving towards everyone in your church, are you showing it? The love of Jesus takes a meal to the family who is struggling and washes the car of the person under pressure; it rolls up its sleeves and gets stuck in.

The disciples weren't a worthy bunch; they were sinful and their backgrounds were messy. And yet Jesus loved them so much that he went to the cross for them. Today, as we share life with those in our church, an equally sinful and messy group (ourselves included), Jesus says to us what he said to his first disciples: 'As I have loved you, so you must love one another.' We are to love those in our local church with a Calvary love. When we do that, we are proof that the gospel is true. Be patient with one another, be kind, be forgiving and bear one another's burdens because people who don't know how much they need God are watching. Cause them to question and to wonder: 'See how these Christians love one another!' Amaze them with God's love in action and stir their hearts for more.

Day 17

Read John 21:1–25
Key verses: John 21:10, 12, 15

. . . .

[10] Jesus said to them, 'Bring some of the fish you have just caught . . . [12] Come and have breakfast.' . . .

[15] When they had finished eating, Jesus said to Simon Peter, 'Simon son of John, do you love me more than these?'

Sights, sounds and smells can reawaken long lost memories and help us to relive past experiences.

No doubt seeing Jesus standing on the shore would have taken the disciples right back to the beginning of their experience with him. It was on that same stretch of beach that Jesus had said, 'Follow me, and I will make you fishers of men' (Matthew 4:19, ESV). Perhaps for Peter that charcoal fire reminded him of the other early morning and the other fire where he had warmed himself as he denied the Lord (John 18:15–18).

Before Jesus can reissue the call to 'follow me' (21:19), he needs to ask Peter a crucial question: 'Do you [truly] love me more than these?' (verse 15). More than what? More than the fishing tackle and the 153 fish? More than his boat, his friends or his former life? To find the answer, remember what Peter was like. He regularly bragged about his superior commitment to the Lord. He measured himself against the other disciples and argued that he was better than they were. It was Peter who said, 'Even if all fall away on account of you, I never will' (Matthew 26:33). This is the man who, when Jesus was about to be arrested, said, 'Why can't I follow you now? I'm ready to go with you, no matter the cost. Just say the word and I'll lay down my life for you' (see Matthew 26:35; Luke 22:33). Before the cross, Peter had been so self-assured, so certain of his love and his loyalty. Yet, when the crunch came and the disciples deserted Jesus, Peter had gone further than them all and denied the Lord with oaths and curses.

By his actions, Peter had shown that he didn't want a crucified saviour. So how did Peter's devotion stand now? Was he ready to love Jesus when Jesus wasn't the type of saviour he wanted? Was he ready to follow the Lord whose body still bore the holes the nails made, the marks of rejection? Was he ready to devote himself to Christ who was labelled a 'failure' because he had gone to a cross?

When we're in church or surrounded by other Christians, it is easy to feel certain of our love and loyalty to Christ. But when Jesus doesn't behave as we want him to, when he doesn't improve our situation or answer our prayers, or when we are branded failures or face rejection because of our association with him, our love is tested. Will we love and trust the real Jesus, not a Jesus of our own making? Will we follow Christ when the road to ultimate victory passes through times of failure and rejection?

Today, pray that through all life's circumstances – even your present troubles – you will be obedient to Jesus and your love for him will continue to grow.

Day 18

Read John 21:1–25
Key verses: John 21:15–17

••

¹⁵ *When they had finished eating, Jesus said to Simon Peter, 'Simon son of John, do you love me more than these?'*

'Yes, Lord,' he said, 'you know that I love you.'

Jesus said, 'Feed my lambs.'

¹⁶ *Again Jesus said, 'Simon son of John, do you love me?'*

He answered, 'Yes, Lord, you know that I love you.'

Jesus said, 'Take care of my sheep.'

¹⁷ *The third time he said to him, 'Simon son of John, do you love me?'*

Peter was hurt because Jesus asked him the third time, 'Do you love me?' He said, 'Lord, you know all things; you know that I love you.'

'You know that I love you!'

Peter's appeal to Jesus' knowledge of him may seem a very strange and shaky basis for his argument. Peter had denied knowing Jesus; there was no recent proof of his love. And yet the 'you' is emphatic in the Greek. Peter is saying to Jesus, 'Lord, you know everything. *You* know that I love you.'

Jesus knows the worst about us and loves us anyway. If he didn't know the worst about me, I might wonder whether, one day, something might turn up that would turn him away from me. We think that about people sometimes. We're afraid that a failure, weakness, sin, bad mistake or terrible action in the past might come to the surface and fracture our relationship. But the Lord Jesus knows absolutely everything that there is to know about us, and he loves us just the same. Nothing will ever surprise him or catch him off guard about us.

It is not just that Jesus knows the worst about us; he also – and this is particularly on Peter's mind – knows the best about us. When people fail in one area of life, we tend to write them off in every area. We begin to view everything they do through the lens of their weakness or failure. We may reach the stage where we question every motive and action of theirs. But the Lord Jesus knows our hearts. Do you feel condemned by others or by your own conscience? The Lord Jesus Christ knows that deep inside you, alongside all the mixed motives (and there are mixed motives), the accumulated junk of diverted affections, the proven frailty and the bad record, there is a genuine but feeble love for him.

As we struggle with sin, the condemnation of others and our own mixed motives, Jesus says, 'I know.' He knows our weak and faltering love. He knows the very worst and best about us but he loves us still.

I am graven on the palms of his hands [Isaiah 49:16]. I am never out of his mind . . . I know him because he first knew me, and continues to know me. He knows me as a friend, one who loves me; and there is no moment when his eye is off me, or his attention distracted from me, and no moment, therefore, when his care falters. (J. I. Packer, *Knowing God*, Hodder & Stoughton, 2005, p. 45)

Day 19

Read John 21:1–25
Key verses: John 21:17, 20–22

....

¹⁷ *The third time he said to him, 'Simon son of John, do you love me?'*

   Peter was hurt because Jesus asked him the third time, 'Do you love me?' He said, 'Lord, you know all things; you know that I love you.'

   Jesus said, 'Feed my sheep.' . . .

²⁰ *Peter turned and saw that the disciple whom Jesus loved was following them . . .* ²¹*When Peter saw him, he asked, 'Lord, what about him?'*

   ²² *Jesus answered, 'If I want him to remain alive until I return, what is that to you? You must follow me.'*

What does love cost?

Three times Jesus asks Peter, 'Do you love me?' Each time, Peter responds positively and Jesus' answers, 'OK, now love my people.' Essentially, whatever our ministry –

teaching, serving, encouraging – ultimately, it is a ministry of love to God's people. And there is a price to pay.

For Peter, that meant crucifixion (John 21:18–19). All followers of Jesus have to die. You may have to die the death of embarrassment as people at college or work mock you for attending church. You may have to die a death as you say no to a wrong relationship you've been enjoying or to a dishonest business practice that has been very profitable.

Being told that we're going to have a difficult time is hard to bear. But human frailty being what it is, we like to know that someone else is going to have it hard, too. Jesus has just told Peter that following him will be costly; he's going to end up dying. So Peter turns round, sees John and asks the Lord, 'What about him? Is he going to have it hard, too? How's he going to die?' Jesus' reply is curt, almost brutal: 'Don't look at John. Follow me. John's form of service, his life experience may be very different from yours, but that's my business. You keep your eyes on me.'

Peter and John's ministries were to follow divergent routes. Similarly, in the church, we all have different experiences. There are rich, poor, healthy and sick. Some will die at a great old age, like John, and others will die in middle life, like Peter. Some will die in their beds; others will die tragically. There's always a danger that we will look at other people and think, 'They've got it better than me!' But Jesus urges us to keep on loving him and his people: '*You* follow me.'

Don't look around at how everyone else is serving God. Stop comparing how he is dealing with them with your situation. Stop measuring your love against theirs. God has placed you where you are, with a unique set of relationships and responsibilities. He has allowed every suffering you face and knows the path you walk. And he calls you to love him – with the love that only you can. No one else can love God as you can in the pain of your particular situation. No one else can offer your joyful sacrifice. Surely, it is true that

Love so amazing, so divine,
demands my soul, my life, my all.
(Isaac Watts, 'When I Survey the Wondrous Cross', 1707)

Romans

The great Reformer Martin Luther described the book of Romans as 'the chief part of the New Testament and the very purest Gospel'.* It is packed with key theological truths by which the apostle Paul lived and died. Romans was probably written by Paul during his third missionary journey, when he was on the way back to Jerusalem, with the collection he'd received for the poverty-stricken believers. In the letter, he is at pains to convey the full scope of God's glorious salvation plan and the future glory awaiting the whole of creation, including us. To this mixed congregation, who had never had a visit from an apostle, Paul carefully sets out the basic truths of the gospel and God's redemption plan for both Jews and Gentiles. He explains why Christians can be confident of God's love, certain that God will conform them to the likeness of Christ, secure in their salvation and the hope of final glory.

---

* Martin Luther, 'Preface to the Epistle to the Romans' (1522), *Works of Martin Luther*, Muhlenberg Press, 1932, vol. 6, p. 447.

Day 20

Read Romans 8:31–39
Key verses: Romans 8:32–34

. . . .

[32] He who did not spare his own Son, but gave him up for us all – how will he not also, along with him, graciously give us all things? [33] Who will bring any charge against those whom God has chosen? It is God who justifies. [34] Who then is the one who condemns? No one. Christ Jesus who died – more than that, who was raised to life – is at the right hand of God and is also interceding for us.

Does God stop loving me when I sin?

When we're feeling wretched about a particular sin we've committed in the past or disappointed with ourselves for giving in to habitual sin, it is easy to imagine God metaphorically throwing up his hands in despair. Surely there must come a point when God looks at our sin and says, 'Enough is enough'?

Paul frames the question differently. He asks, 'Do you think the living God who sent his Son to die for you – that's the hard part if you like – will not finish the job and take you to be with him for ever?' (See verse 32.) God loves you. He will not let you go. Yes, we will fail. We will commit terrible sins, and there will be all sorts of accusers – the devil, individuals we have wronged, even our own consciences – but, however grievous our sins, the prosecution cannot win because God has already delivered the verdict: we are justified (see verse 33).

The moment we sin, we can imagine Satan accusing us before God. Then Jesus stands and speaks to God on our behalf (see verse 34). He says, 'Father, I died for their sin. I've dealt with it already. I faced your wrath; I faced the judgment.' If you are trusting in Christ today and believe Jesus died for your sin, then you can be sure that Jesus has dealt with it and you are clean before a holy God.

> The moment we believe, God imputes Christ's perfect performance to us as if it were our own and adopts us into His family. In other words, God can say to us just as He once said to Christ, 'You are my Son, whom I love; with you I am well pleased.'
> (Timothy Keller, *The Freedom of Self-Forgetfulness*, 2012, 10Publishing, p. 40)

Fallen, anxious sinners are limitless in their capacity to perceive reasons for Jesus to cast them out. We are factories of fresh resistances to Christ's love ... [But we] cannot present a reason for Christ to finally close off his heart to his own sheep. No such reason exists. Every human friend has a limit. If we offend enough, if a relationship gets damaged enough, if we betray enough, we are cast out. The walls go up. With Christ, our sins and weaknesses are the very resumé items that qualify us to approach him. Nothing but coming to him is required – first at conversion and then a thousand times thereafter until we are with him upon death.

(Dane Ortlund, *Gentle and Lowly*, Crossway, 2020, pp. 63–64)

Day 21

Read Romans 8:31–39
Key verses: Romans 8:35, 37

....

> 35 *Who shall separate us from the love of Christ? Shall trouble or hardship or persecution or famine or nakedness or danger or sword? . . . * 37 *No, in all these things we are more than conquerors through him who loved us.*

'If God really loved me, he wouldn't let me suffer like this!'

When our bodies are wracked with pain and our minds are flooded with anxiety, depression or bitter disappointment, we may find ourselves doubting God's love. But Paul is clear: just as our sins cannot separate us from God's love (Day 20), neither can our circumstances.

He asks, 'Who shall separate us from the love of Christ?' Then he lists all sorts of possible candidates: trouble, hardship, persecution, famine, nakedness, danger or sword (martyrdom). Why does Paul ask these questions if he doesn't imagine that they could happen to Christians? We can't have a naive spirituality that leads us to think, 'If I'm really faithful to God, terrible things will never happen to me.' Paul's point is that these things may happen. You might face every one of them. Christians loved by God can face terrible suffering.

He quotes from the Old Testament: 'For your sake we face death all day long; we are considered as sheep to be slaughtered' (verse 36). Believers are crying out, 'We have been faithful to you, Lord, and it's because of our faithfulness to you that we are suffering, that we are like sheep to be slaughtered.' Suffering can happen not just because of the general circumstances of living in a fallen world; it can happen even because of our faithfulness to Jesus. Perhaps you are a pastor desperately trying to preach Bible truth but your congregation or people in the community don't like what they are hearing and want to get rid of you. Perhaps you are being faithful to Christ at work; you stand up for him and colleagues are giving you the cold shoulder. Maybe you are the only Christian in your family and you feel alienated. These things can happen.

But, when suffering comes, it cannot separate us from the love of God in Christ. Paul says, '*In all these things* we are more than conquerors through him who loved us' (verse 37, emphasis added). Literally, we are super-conquerors, not by escaping the suffering but by being in it and going through it. No doubt we will be battered and bruised, physically and emotionally, but we will come through because all things, including our suffering, are leading us to glory.

Whatever your suffering – betrayal by a close friend, ill health, loss of a loved one, loneliness, miscarriage, abuse at work because of your faith – be assured of God's love for you:

'Though the mountains be shaken
    and the hills be removed,
yet my unfailing love for you will not be shaken
    nor my covenant of peace be removed,'
    says the Lord, who has compassion on you.
(Isaiah 54:10)

Day 22

Read Romans 8:31–39
Key verses: Romans 8:38–39

....

38 *For I am convinced that neither death nor life, neither angels nor demons, neither the present nor the future, nor any powers,* 39 *neither height nor depth, nor anything else in all creation, will be able to separate us from the love of God that is in Christ Jesus our Lord.*

If sin and suffering can't separate us from God's love, can anything else?

Paul gives a comprehensive list to answer this question with a resounding no!

'Neither death nor life': death may separate us from one another but not from God, and life won't either, with all its eventualities. 'Neither angels nor demons': in other words, no spiritual forces will have sway in our lives; they are powerless before Christ. 'Neither the present nor the future': you may be going through a bad patch now – you are lonely, depressed and discouraged; you may not feel God's love but he is with you. What is your greatest fear as you face the future? Perhaps the loss of friends, family, job, reputation or your mind? All those things could happen. You could lose them all but, in Christ, you cannot lose God. 'Nor any powers', whether spiritual or temporal, can come between us and God. Oppressive regimes can deprive Christians of property and freedom, even our lives, but they cannot separate us from God's love. 'Neither height nor depth': we can go up to the moon or down to the bottom of the sea, or into a difficult non-Christian family situation or a secular workplace – it doesn't matter where we go because God is there. Then, just in case Paul has missed anything, there is a catch-all phrase: 'nor anything else in all creation'. Nothing 'will be able to separate us from the love of God that is in Christ Jesus'.

Other human beings may let us down, even the best of them. It's only in Christ that we find the eternal security we long for. And when he says, 'I will always love you,' he means it.

> The soul that on Jesus has leaned for repose,
> I will not, I will not, desert to its foes;
> that soul, though all hell should endeavour to shake,
> I'll never, no never, no never forsake!
> (Anon., 'How Firm a Foundation', 1787)

Is it a small thing in your eyes to be loved by God – to be the son, the spouse, the love, the delight of the King of glory? Christian, believe this, and think about it: you will be eternally embraced in the arms of the love which was from everlasting, and will extend to everlasting – of the love which brought the Son of God's love from heaven to earth, from earth to the cross, from the cross to the grave, from the grave to glory – that love which was weary, hungry, tempted, scorned, scourged, buffeted, spat upon, crucified, pierced – which fasted, prayed, taught, healed, wept, sweated, bled, died. That love will eternally embrace you.

(Richard Baxter, *The Practical Works of the Late Reverend and Pious Mr Richard Baxter*, 1707, vol. 3, p. 21)

1 John and Revelation

1 John

John, the apostle and author of the Gospel of John and Revelation, wrote this letter to be circulated among the churches in the province of Asia, where an early form of Gnosticism was infiltrating. This heresy taught that the spirit is entirely good and matter is entirely evil. In Gnosticism, what you did with your body was of no concern, so breaking God's law was of no consequence and thus a lack of morality ruled. Salvation was seen as an escape from the body, not by faith in Jesus Christ but by possessing special knowledge. John wrote to oppose this false teaching and assure believers: 'I write these things to you who believe in the name of the Son of God so that you may know that you have eternal life' (5:13). He points to Jesus' death as the grounds for our unshakeable confidence in God's love and our salvation. John also encourages believers that love for one another is the overflow and evidence of a life transformed by faith in God.

Revelation

As early as the end of the first century, false teaching and internal division were rife in the church. The Roman emperor Domitian had instigated another wave of persecution against those who would not worship him as lord. The apostle John, exiled on the island of Patmos, urged believers to resist the demands of the emperor, knowing that God was with them and that, one day soon, they would be vindicated. Written in an apocalyptic style, the book of Revelation is full of highly symbolic visions that can seem strange to us. We won't understand every detail, but the message of God's sovereignty and the certainty of Christ's triumphant return comes across strongly. John wrote to encourage believers of every generation to hold fast to their faith, confident in God's love and their glorious future.

Day 23

Read 1 John 3:10–18
Key verses: 1 John 3:10–11

∙∙∙

> ¹⁰*This is how we know who the children of God are and who the children of the devil are: anyone who does not do what is right is not God's child, nor is anyone who does not love their brother and sister.*
> ¹¹*For this is the message you heard from the beginning: we should love one another.*

What is the evidence of genuine Christianity?

The New Testament repeatedly tells us that the two marks of authenticity are our faith in Jesus Christ and our love for God and other believers (Colossians 1:3–4; Ephesians 1:15; 1 Thessalonians 1:3).

If we are children of God, we cannot disguise who our Father is because our habitual behaviour towards one another will demonstrate it. It is the nature of God to love, so the centrepiece of the law, which reflects his nature, is this: 'Love the Lord your God with all your heart . . . Love your neighbour as yourself' (Matthew 22:37–39). It was the new commandment Jesus gave his disciples, and no one can come into a real personal relationship with a God who is love without being transformed into a loving person.

By contrast, Cain was characterized by hatred, like his father the evil one, and he murdered his brother (Genesis 4:1–8). The root of the problem was not just that Cain disliked his brother; there was also a moral battle, which Cain lost. Cain offered God his crops instead of a blood sacrifice, the means God had determined for entering into his presence. In that sense, Cain's actions were evil (1 John 3:12); he would not accept God's authority, which is why his sacrifice was rejected. John's point is that when individuals determine to go their own way, when they follow the evil one as their father, the result is always disintegration in one's personal life and, eventually, in society.

Cain hated Abel's obedience, so we shouldn't be surprised if the world hates obedient Christians, however much we seek to express God's love (verse 13). At one time we, too, followed the example of our father, the devil. But Christians have passed out of that sphere (verse 14). How can we be sure we belong to God's family? Because we love our brothers and sisters in Christ. We have one Father and we belong to one another because we belong to him. The mark of our new lives as believers is this love for one another.

It would be easier if the evidence of our new lives in Christ were marked by the worldly things we avoid or the church ministry we do. But 'from the beginning', love for one another has been the mark of those who belong to Christ. Love is not something that can be regulated or ticked off our 'to do' list; rather, it is the overflow of a life transformed by faith in God. It is no wonder that the refrain of the New Testament and God's message for us today is still to 'love all of God's family . . . Yet we urge you, brothers and sisters, to do so more and more' (1 Thessalonians 4:10).

Day 24

Read 1 John 3:10–18
Key verses: 1 John 3:16–17

....

> *16 This is how we know what love is: Jesus Christ laid down his life for us. And we ought to lay down our lives for our brothers and sisters. 17 If anyone has material possessions and sees a brother or sister in need but has no pity on them, how can the love of God be in that person?*

What you believe affects how you behave.

Cain's hatred of Abel led to murder. In fact, anyone who hates is a murderer; they share the same moral character, which is incompatible with being a child of God. The devil's family reveals its hatred by taking life. By stark contrast, divine love revealed its character when Jesus laid down his life for us on the cross. Love doesn't take another's life in thought or deed; it gives its own life so that others may live. As Jesus said, 'I am the good shepherd. The good shepherd lays down his life for the sheep' (John 10:11).

This love, not in word but in deed, is the sort of action that God looks for in his children. John links belief and behaviour together: the truth that Christ died for me inevitably leads to the outworking of that truth in love for my brothers and sisters (1 John 3:16). God's love was unique. We cannot die for one another so that we may be forgiven. But if that unique love has brought us to the point of true repentance and faith in Jesus, then the love we have begun to recognize will be reproduced in our lives. In Jesus, we see that love in perfection and, if faith is real love, it will not be beyond us. There will be evidence of its beginning to grow in our love for one another.

It may come as a shock how practical this love is. The proof of genuine Christianity is not just that I sing songs of praise but also that I am prepared to give without any thought of return, just as Jesus gave; it's that I am prepared to give without first weighing up the worthiness of the person who receives. A love like this will have an impact on my diary, finances, possessions and energy. It is an attitude of mind that will result in specific, sacrificial action. God is love so the more we receive the life of God, the more that life will flood into us and overflow to others.

Love calls you beyond the borders of your own wants, needs, and feelings . . . Love calls you to lay down your life in ways that are concrete and specific. Love calls you to serve, to wait, to give, to suffer, to forgive, and to do all these things again and again. Love calls you to be silent when you want to speak, and to speak when you would like to be silent . . . Love calls you to stop when you really want to continue, and it calls you to continue when you feel like stopping . . . Love again and again calls you away from your instincts and your comfort. Love always requires personal sacrifice. Love calls you to give up your life.

(Paul David Tripp, *What Did You Expect?*, IVP, 2010, p. 188)

Day 25

Read 1 John 3:11–24
Key verses: 1 John 3:19–20

....

19This is how we know that we belong to the truth and how we set our hearts at rest in his presence: 20if our hearts condemn us, we know that God is greater than our hearts, and he knows everything.

Do you feel guilty that you don't love other Christians enough? Do you look at the high standard God has for loving others and feel so inadequate that you wonder whether you are truly saved at all?

John is aware that genuine Christians' hearts often condemn them. We know our own inner motives and how often our love for our brothers and sisters falls far short of what it ought to be. There are individual believers whom we struggle to love.

But the hearts that condemn us can be set at rest in the presence of God. John doesn't deny the condemnation of our hearts but he encourages us to see that God knows more (verse 20). This doesn't mean that God overlooks our failures; he knows them better than we do. God also knows that the measure of love we do have is irrefutable evidence that we are truly saved, that we have crossed from death to life (verse 14). Yes, we are imperfect. Our hearts cry out for more consistent love but that doesn't destroy our assurance; it confirms it. It shows that we are children of God and that we have begun to love our brothers and sisters. The eighteenth-century Methodist preacher and evangelist John Wesley was said to frequently pray: 'Lord, cure me of my intermittent piety and make me thoroughly Christian.'

When we face the crisis of a condemning heart, our rest is found in the certain knowledge that we do belong to the truth. We can commit ourselves to a God who knows us far better than we know ourselves, and whose work of grace and love in our lives is not determined by our feelings but by his unchanging eternal purpose of faithfulness and love.

We often feel disappointed and ashamed that our love for others is so feeble. But God is not surprised and his love towards us is not determined by it:

There is tremendous relief in knowing that his love to me is utterly realistic, based at every point on prior knowledge of the worst about me, so that no discovery now can disillusion him about me, in the way I am so often disillusioned about myself, and quench his determination to bless me.

(J. I. Packer, *Knowing God*, Hodder & Stoughton, 2005, p. 45)

Today, trust God's Word and his knowledge of you. As you ask God for a more consistent love for him and for others, do not listen to your condemning heart or subjective feelings but find 'rest in [God's] presence', delighting in the truth that you belong to him.

Day 26

Read 1 John 3:11–24
Key verses: 1 John 3:21–23

. . . .

> [21] *Dear friends, if our hearts do not condemn us, we have confidence before God* [22] *and receive from him anything we ask, because we keep his commands and do what pleases him.* [23] *And this is his command: to believe in the name of his Son, Jesus Christ, and to love one another as he commanded us.*

Are you a confident Christian?

John's point is not that there are two types of Christians: those who are confident and approach God boldly, and those whose hearts condemn them for their lack of love. Rather, our condemning hearts find rest when we know that God loves us, although our love for him is weak and faint. When we realize that God's love for us doesn't depend on our love for him, there is a confidence (and a humility, too) in speaking to him face to face. Grasping how very much God loves us can transform our prayer lives.

The fact that God treats us like dearly loved children by answering our prayers is further evidence of his love for us (verse 22). We keep on receiving because we keep on asking in his will, and we do that because we keep on obeying him. Imagine our relationship with God as a spiral staircase: the more we let God's Word fill our minds, direct our wills and transform our affections, the more we please God, and the more we are sure of his love and are confident to approach him.

To increase our assurance of salvation even more, John coalesces all these commands one final time into one great statement: 'This is his command: to believe in the name of his Son, Jesus Christ, and to love one another as he commanded us' (verse 23). What does God want from us? Believing and loving. Belief here implies a definite, once-and-for-all action in the past, but love is in the present continuous tense. Believing 'in the name of . . . Jesus' is more than just believing in orthodox theology. It means believing in the person and believing that Jesus has the power signified by his name, which enables us to trust in him. To believe in the name of Jesus is to believe in his nature and that he is God, the Son of God, the Saviour and Lord. The natural outcome of that sort of believing is obedience in loving others. And that daily, detailed obedience is an increasing assurance of this life of Christ within by the power of the Holy Spirit (verse 24).

Believing in Jesus and loving others – our confidence as believers is inextricably linked to these two commands, which cannot be uncoupled.

> You cannot truly love others unless you are convinced that God's love for you is unconditional, based solely on the merit of Christ, not on your performance. John said, 'We love because he first loved us' (1 John 4:19). Our love, either to God or to others, can only be a response to His love for us.
>
> (Jerry Bridges, *Transforming Grace*, NavPress, 1991, p. 132)

Day 27

Read 1 John 4:7–21
Key verses: 1 John 4:8–12

. . . .

8 Whoever does not love does not know God, because God is love. 9 This is how God showed his love among us: he sent his one and only Son into the world that we might live through him. 10 This is love: not that we loved God, but that he loved us and sent his Son as an atoning sacrifice for our sins. 11 Dear friends, since God so loved us, we also ought to love one another. 12 No one has ever seen God; but if we love one another, God lives in us and his love is made complete in us.

God is love – what a claim!

John isn't pointing to a quality that God possesses; he is making a statement about the essence of his being. This is one reason why God is revealed in Scripture as Trinity. At the very heart of God, there is a dynamic relationship of love. The Father loves the Son, the Son the Father and the Spirit the Son. To imagine that God does not love us is to deny his very nature. His love doesn't depend on our worthiness or even the response of those being loved; he loves us because he is love (see Deuteronomy 7:7–8).

The cross of Christ demonstrates the extent of God's love (1 John 4:9–10). He had only one Son whom he sent into a rebellious world to redeem and reconcile us to God. He sent him to die as a sacrifice that atones, which meant taking upon himself all the guilt of sinful men and women. It also meant carrying the wrath of God, until he quenched it in himself, so that we would not have to face it. This is love: a love that sacrifices, forgives, that goes deeper than sorrow, sin and death itself; a love that restores and reconciles.

The mark of the reality of Christ's love is seen in the transformed lives of his people (see verse 12). Once we begin to see the greatness of the love of God that Jesus showed by giving his life for us, we are motivated towards that sort of love. The world should be able to look at the church and say, 'I can't see God. I don't understand about his love, but when I see these Christians loving one another, I begin to understand.' The Word was made flesh once perfectly in Christ, but the invisible God has a body on this earth; his love is to be seen in that body, and to be content with anything else is to deny the gospel.

Today, meditate on and praise God for his love.

To know that from eternity my Maker, foreseeing my sin, foreloved me and resolved to save me, though it would be at the cost of Calvary; to know that the divine Son was appointed from eternity to be my Saviour, and that in love he became man for me and died for me and now lives to intercede for me and will one day come in person to take me home; to know that the Lord 'who loved me and gave himself for me' . . . has by his Spirit raised me from spiritual death to life-giving union and communion with himself, and has promised to hold me fast and never let me go – this is knowledge that brings overwhelming gratitude and joy.

(J. I. Packer, *Celebrating the Saving Work of God: Volume 1*, Regent College Publishing, 2008, pp. 158–159).

Day 28

Read Revelation 2:1–7
Key verses: Revelation 2:3–4

···

³You have persevered and have endured hardships for my name, and have not grown weary.

⁴Yet I hold this against you: you have forsaken the love you had at first.

Have you forsaken your first love?

In about AD 62, Paul wrote to the church in Ephesus. He prayed for the believers to know what it meant for Christ to be at home and living in their hearts by faith. He prayed for them to know, in their personal experience, the love of Christ, which surpasses all intellectual understanding.

I pray that you, being rooted and established in love, may have power, together with all the Lord's holy people, to grasp how wide and long and high and deep is the love of Christ, and to know this love that surpasses

knowledge – that you may be filled to the measure of all
the fullness of God.
(Ephesians 3:17–19)

He pleaded with them to live a life of love and set before
them the standard: 'live a life of love, just as Christ loved
us and gave himself up for us as a fragrant offering and
sacrifice to God' (5:2).

More than thirty years had passed since that exhortation
to 'live a life of love', and what do we find? In John's
vision, the risen Lord commended the Ephesian believers
for their service, good deeds and doctrinal purity, but his
complaint was that they had 'forsaken the love they had
at first'. Perhaps it happened so slowly that they failed to
notice their drift away from loving God wholeheartedly.
But the other commendations counted for nothing if
there was no love.

Have you left your first love? Do you remember, when
you were first converted, how thrilled you were to read
your Bible? Do you remember going to church and drink-
ing in what the preacher was saying? Do you remember
how hurt you were when you discovered that Christians
were not quite the people they ought to be? Do you
remember how keen you were to share the gospel and
tell other people about how you became a Christian? Do

you remember going to Communion and being so moved thinking about Jesus dying for you?

And now what? When did you last speak to somebody about Jesus? When did you last spend time alone with God in prayer and Bible study? When was the last time you went to church with a sense of expectation that God would speak to you through his Word? The novelty is bound to have worn off if you have been a Christian a while, but the love need not.

Passion for Christ is not reserved exclusively for new Christians. In fact, as we mature our love should deepen because we've passed through difficult circumstances; we've found God sufficient and we've experienced his faithfulness, despite our sinfulness. Pray that, in a fresh way, you would 'know this love [of Christ] that surpasses knowledge' and, with a sense of joyful gratitude overflowing from that, you would 'live a life of love, just as Christ loved us and gave himself up for us' (Ephesians 3:19; 5:2).

Day 29

Read: Revelation 2:1–7
Key verses: Revelation 2:3–4

....

³You have persevered and have endured hardships for my name, and have not grown weary.
⁴Yet I hold this against you: you have forsaken the love you had at first.

How do I know if I truly love the Lord Jesus?

Love is not a gushy feeling; it is not mere sentiment. Gratitude is at the heart of love. We are grateful for what God has done, for what he has given us and for who he is. When we love someone, we don't just make empty declarations; we show our gratitude.

If we love people, we think about them. Do you think about Jesus often? It is easy to be so consumed by thoughts of doctrine, ministry and church duties that we don't actually think about Jesus. We are pressed down and weighed under with all the responsibilities we carry for the Christian cause, but we don't think about him.

When we love people, we are eager to hear their voices. Are you listening for the voice of Jesus? Are you eager to study God's Word to hear from him?

If we love people, we do not like to think of their going away and we look forward to their return. Are you longing for the Lord Jesus to come back soon? Does your heart echo the words at the end of Revelation: 'Come, Lord Jesus' (22:20)?

When we love people, we are anxious to know what will please them so that we can do it. Are you longing to know what brings God pleasure? Do you read your Bible, not just to sign off on the task but also because you are keen to find out what you can do to please God?

When we love people, we are keen to introduce them to others. Are you passionate about telling others about Jesus or have too many knock-backs and awkward conversations meant you have given up sharing the gospel?

When we love people, we are concerned for their good name. We cannot bear people talking about them in a way that is detrimental. Are you concerned about Christ's reputation and the way he is spoken of by others?

When we love people, we do not find it hard to trust them. Sometimes our trust in Jesus wavers. We allow doubts about his good purposes and bitterness about disappointments to swamp our thinking. Grievances over the way the Lord has dealt with us creep into our hearts and minds. That sense of injustice and unfairness festers until, before we know it, we have forsaken our first love.

Which of these markers of love do you recognize in your own life? Don't let bitterness, busyness or familiarity choke your love for God. He is your Everlasting Father (Isaiah 9:6), Chief Shepherd (1 Peter 5:4) and Rock (1 Samuel 2:2). Keep him at the centre of your thoughts and attention for he is 'altogether lovely' (Song of Solomon 5:16).

Day 30

Read Revelation 2:1–7
Key verse: Revelation 2:5

....

⁵*Consider how far you have fallen! Repent and do the things you did at first. If you do not repent, I will come to you and remove your lampstand from its place.*

Were you once known as a very keen Christian but, now, you are lukewarm?

When Paul wrote to the Ephesian church, he commended them: 'Ever since I heard about your faith in the Lord Jesus and your love for all God's people, I have not stopped giving thanks for you, remembering you in my prayers' (Ephesians 1:15–16).

Now the risen Christ calls the believers to 'consider how far [they] have fallen!' Like the Ephesians, the first step is for us to admit our current state and recognize how far we have fallen. Once, the Lord heard our love rising to him in grateful praise; now, he just hears our pattered prayers with no freshness left. The second step is to repent. This means turning away from our sin, and trusting the Lord to cleanse us from our lovelessness and give us the strength to go on living as we ought to live.

The third step, after considering how far we have fallen and repenting, is to 'do the things [we] did at first'. We must do again what love made us do in the first instance, so that we may learn to love again: read the Bible and spend unhurried time with God. We are to seek his wisdom about those to whom we ought to witness, ask for help when those 'first things' have become routine, and come back to him in sheer dependence like newborn Christians.

If we have substituted activity for adoration, busyness for communion and duty for devotion, we must tell the Lord. If our acts of worship have become habitual rather than heartfelt and we have 'forsaken the love [we] had at first', God is waiting to meet us and welcome us back. His mercy, love and compassion for us are overwhelming. He will pick us up despite the people we have put off with our hardness of heart, despite those to whom we have misrepresented him with our lukewarm Christianity.

God longs to give us something we can never whip up within our own hearts – the love which is a gift of God and the fruit of the Holy Spirit. He delights to impart that love in fullness and freshness as we bow before him and confess our need.

Is this message really for us? Yes! John says, 'Whoever has ears, let them hear what the Spirit says to the churches' (Revelation 2:7). God has made the way back to him clear; he has set out a three-step plan for how to do it. And now, like the father in the story of the prodigal son (Luke 15:11–32), he stands with his arms open wide, ready to welcome us home. What is holding you back?

For further study

If you would like to read more about God's love and ours, you might find the following selection of books helpful.

Books about God's love:

- Julian Hardyman, *Jesus, Lover of My Soul: Fresh Pathways to Spiritual Passion* (IVP, 2020).

- Patrick Mitchel, *The Message of Love*, The Bible Speaks Today (IVP, 2019).

- Dane Ortlund, *Gentle and Lowly: The Heart of Christ for Sinners and Sufferers* (Crossway, 2020).

- Phil Ryken, *Loving the Way Jesus Loves* (IVP, 2012).

- Martin Salter, *So Loved: 26 Words that Can Change Your Life* (IVP, 2021).

Books about love and relationships:

- Paul E. Miller, *A Loving Life: In a World of Broken Relationships* (IVP, 2014).

- Jason Roach, *Swipe Up: A Better Way to Do Love, Sex and Relationships* (The Good Book Company, 2019).

A book about loving other Christians:

• Tony Merida, *Love Your Church: 8 Great Things about Being a Church Member* (The Good Book Company, 2021).

Keswick Ministries

Our purpose

Keswick Ministries exists to inspire and equip Christians to love and live for Christ in his world.

God's purpose is to bring his blessing to all the nations of the world (Genesis 12:3). That promise of blessing, which touches every aspect of human life, is ultimately fulfilled through the life, death, resurrection, ascension and future return of Christ. All the people of God are called to participate in his missionary purposes, wherever he may place them. The central vision of Keswick Ministries is to see the people of God equipped, inspired and refreshed to fulfil that calling, directed and guided by God's Word in the power of his Spirit, for the glory of his Son.

Our priorities

There are three fundamental priorities which shape all that we do as we look to serve the local church.

• *Hearing God's Word*: the Scriptures are the foundation for the church's life, growth and mission, and Keswick Ministries is committed to preach and teach God's

Word in a way that is faithful to Scripture and relevant to Christians of all ages and backgrounds.

- *Becoming like God's Son*: from its earliest days, the Keswick movement has encouraged Christians to live godly lives in the power of the Spirit, to grow in Christlikeness and to live under his Lordship in every area of life. This is God's will for his people in every culture and generation.

- *Serving God's mission*: the authentic response to God's Word is obedience to his mission, and the inevitable result of Christlikeness is sacrificial service. Keswick Ministries seeks to encourage committed discipleship in family life, work and society, and energetic engagement in the cause of world mission.

Our ministry

- *Keswick Convention*. The Convention attracts some 12,000 to 15,000 Christians from the UK and around the world to Keswick every summer. It provides Bible teaching for all ages, vibrant worship, a sense of unity across generations and denominations, and an inspirational call to serve Christ in the world. It caters for children of all ages and has a strong youth and young adult programme. And it all takes place in the beautiful

Lake District – a perfect setting for rest, recreation and refreshment.

- *Keswick fellowship*. For more than 140 years, the work of Keswick has affected churches worldwide, not just through individuals being changed but also through Bible conventions that originate or draw their inspiration from the Keswick Convention. Today, there is a network of events that share Keswick Ministries' priorities across the UK and in many parts of Europe, Asia, North America, Australia, Africa and the Caribbean. Keswick Ministries is committed to strengthening the network in the UK and beyond through prayer, news and co-operative activity.

- *Keswick teaching and training*. Keswick Ministries is developing a range of inspiring, Bible-centred teaching and training that focuses on equipping believers for 'whole-of-life' discipleship. This builds on the same concern that started the Convention, that all Christians live godly lives in the power of the Spirit in all spheres of life in God's world. Some of the smaller and more intensive events focus on equipping attendees, while others focus on inspiring them. Some are for pastors, others for those in different forms of church leadership, while many are for any Christian. The aim of all the courses is for the participants to return home refreshed to serve.

- *Keswick resources.* Keswick Ministries produces a range of books, devotionals, study guides and digital resources to inspire and equip the church to live for Christ. The printed resources focus on the core foundations of Christian life and mission, and help the people of God in their walk with Christ. The digital resources make teaching and sung worship from the Keswick Convention available in a variety of ways.

Our unity

The Keswick movement worldwide has adopted a key Pauline statement to describe its gospel inclusivity: 'All one in Christ Jesus' (Galatians 3:28). Keswick Ministries works with evangelicals from a wide variety of church backgrounds, on the understanding that they share a commitment to the essential truths of the Christian faith as set out in our statement of belief.

Our contact details

T: 017687 80075
E: info@keswickministries.org
W: www.keswickministries.org
Mail: Keswick Ministries, Rawnsley Centre, Main Street, Keswick, Cumbria CA12 5NP, England

Food for the Journey THEMES

The **Food for the Journey: Themes** series offers daily devotions from much loved Bible teachers at the Keswick Convention, exploring how particular themes are woven through the Bible and what we can learn from them today. In a convenient, pocket-sized format, these little books are ideal to accompany you wherever you go.

Available in the series

Confident
978 1 78974 190 2
'A beautiful collection.'
Elinor Magowan

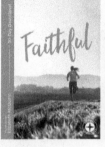

The Cross
978 1 78974 191 9
'A must-read.'
Gavin Calver

Faithful
978 1 78974 341 8
'Gripping.'
Sharon Hastings

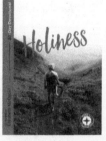

Holiness
978 1 78974 196 4
'Life-giving.'
Marcus Honeysett

Hope
978 1 78974 194 0
'Thought-provoking.'
Linda Allcock

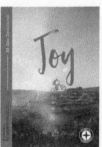

Joy
978 1 78974 163 6
'A rich feast!'
Edrie Mallard

Persevere
978 1 78974 102 5
'Full of essential theology.'
Catherine Campbell

Pray
978 1 78974 169 8
'The ideal reboot.'
Julian Hardyman

Available from your local Christian bookshop or **www.ivpbooks.com**

Related titles from IVP

Food for the Journey

The Food for the Journey series offers daily devotionals from well-loved Bible teachers at the Keswick Convention in an ideal pocket-sized format – to accompany you wherever you go.

Available in the series

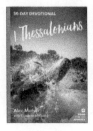

1 Thessalonians

Alec Motyer with

Elizabeth McQuoid

978 1 78359 439 9

2 Timothy

Michael Baughen with

Elizabeth McQuoid

978 1 78359 438 2

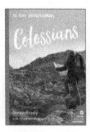

Colossians

Steve Brady with

Elizabeth McQuoid

978 1 78359 722 2

Ezekiel

Liam Goligher with

Elizabeth McQuoid

978 1 78359 603 4

Habakkuk

Jonathan Lamb with

Elizabeth McQuoid

978 1 78359 652 2

Hebrews

Charles Price with

Elizabeth McQuoid

978 1 78359 611 9

James

Stuart Briscoe with

Elizabeth McQuoid

978 1 78359 523 5

John 14 – 17

Simon Manchester with

Elizabeth McQuoid

978 1 78359 495 5

Available from your local Christian bookshop or **www.ivpbooks.com**

Food for the Journey

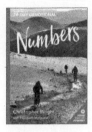   

Numbers	Revelation 1 - 3	Romans 5 - 8	Ruth
Christopher Wright with Elizabeth McQuoid	Paul Mallard with Elizabeth McQuoid	John Stott with Elizabeth McQuoid	Alistair Begg with Elizabeth McQuoid
978 1 78359 720 8	978 1 78359 712 3	978 1 78359 718 5	978 1 78359 525 9

Praise for the series

'This devotional series is biblically rich, theologically deep and full of wisdom . . . I recommend it highly.' **Becky Manley Pippert, speaker, author of** Out of the Saltshaker and into the World **and creator of the Live/Grow/ Know course and series of books**

'These devotional guides are excellent tools.' **John Risbridger, Minister and Team Leader, Above Bar Church, Southampton**

'These bite-sized banquets . . . reveal our loving Father weaving the loose and messy ends of our everyday lives into his beautiful, eternal purposes in Christ.' **Derek Burnside, Principal, Capernwray Bible School**

'I would highly recommend this series of 30-day devotional books to anyone seeking a tool that will help [him or her] to gain a greater love of Scripture, or just simply . . . to do something out of devotion. Whatever your motivation, these little books are a must-read.' **Claud Jackson,** Youthwork **Magazine**